Build Your Authority Platform

By
Marc Guberti

Your Free Gift

As a way of thanking you for your purchase, I am offering you a free ticket to the Content Marketing Success Summit.

The Content Marketing Success Summit showcases an ever growing list of speakers who will teach you how to create, promote, and optimize your content—and use that content to generate a full-time income.

If you are interested in achieving a full-time income from your content brand, then I recommend getting your free ticket for the **Content Marketing Success Summit** which contains the insights that will allow you to reach the next level.

contentmarketingsuccesssummit.com

Table Of Contents

Introduction

YouTube is the top social network to place your videos and grow your business. It's no wonder so many creators upload their content to YouTube. In any given minute, there's over 500 hours of video getting uploaded to YouTube. YouTube also has over 1 billion users ever since its humble beginning on April 23, 2005, when the first video was uploaded to YouTube.

With so much popularity, some believe the platform has become oversaturated and success isn't possible for the new creator on the block. That's just not true, and the data and examples prove it.

It's still possible to take your channel from 0 to 100,000 subscribers in a year. Is it hard? Oh yes, but there are people who do it to this day. While that's more of an exception than the rule, seeing some YouTubers achieve these results shows the platform is still filled with opportunity for new and seasoned creators alike.

I understand how frustrating it can be to grow a YouTube channel. Before I became consistent on YouTube, I was on and off with the platform. If you don't know how to leverage the platform, growth will be slow and the money won't be there.

In this book, I will help you grow your channel and start making money from your YouTube videos. It's possible for any creator to make a big splash on YouTube. The question boils down to how much work you want to put in to make it happen.

If you are ready to make the big splash on YouTube and massively expand your brand, keep reading.

Getting Clear On Your Brand

The first step to building an authority platform is to get clear on the basics. What is your brand? What's your message? What are the values that you stand for?

These aren't the types of questions that immediately translate into visibility and revenue. However, these are the types of questions you need to ask yourself now. It's easy to focus on visibility and revenue and lose sight of what you're actually trying to build and the purpose behind your work in the first place.

An authority platform gives you the ability to impact a specific type of person in a specific way. Some people, like myself, coach people on how to launch, grow, and monetize their podcasts. With this authority platform, I impact people who want to start their podcasts or better leverage their existing ones.

I also believe that age is not a limit to success and emphasize this message in my work. I started my first blog when I was

11 and want young people to know they can start pursuing their dreams now instead of waiting until they get out of college.

This context matters because it has impacted who I've become and the type of authority platform I have built. Context matters when you build your authority platform.

Context doesn't matter if you're trying to build "just another" platform. There are too many social media experts who aren't social media experts.

Furthermore, there are too many social media experts who are just social media experts. The experts who blend their messages with each other never truly stand out.

I have over half a million followers across my social media accounts. However, being known as a social media expert doesn't do anything for me. It's more valuable for me to be known as Marc than it is to be known as a social media expert.

People know who Gary Vaynerchuk is. He doesn't have to tell you he is a social media expert. Anyone who follows Gary *knows* that he is a social media expert. That's the difference between having a moniker and having a brand that turns into an authority platform.

But how do you get people to *know* you versus having the moniker but not standing out amongst the other people who possess the same moniker? If you know a little bit about Gary, you know he pushes out messages like hustle hard, love the process more than the result, and have a ton of gratitude. You might also know he wants to own the NY Jets someday.

No other social media experts embody those messages and truly amplify them as much as him. Every day, you'll always find a few posts on Gary's Instagram that match up with those messages.

Every appearance I get, I amplify the message that age is not a limit to success. This was the core message even when I was starting out and didn't have a platform yet. This is the important stuff to figure out before you build your authority platform so you become more relatable to your core audience and easier for them to remember.

Gary has it set up where some people in his community will think of him when they look up at the clouds in the sky or look down at the dirt on the ground. People like me keep talking about Gary Vaynerchuk because we keep thinking about him and seeing him in action.

You don't get that just by being another social media expert. Let your personality, values, hobbies, and everything else about you truly shine. People may like your content, but when they love you as a person, that's when the magic happens.

Getting Clear On What Type Of Content You Will Focus On

The baseline of all authority platforms is the content. If Gary Vaynerchuk stopped producing content, people would soon forget about him unless someone else amplified his brand and messages for him.

Content is the starting point, but there's never truly a time when you stop producing content. Whether you publish weekly blog posts or daily podcast episodes, producing content keeps you relevant and in your community's frame of mind.

Ideally, you could create a surplus of content for each of the major formats (written content, video content, audio content, and visual content). However, this is not possible for most people, especially in the beginning of the journey.

You should start by creating content that you feel the most comfortable creating. When I started, blogging was my preference. Over 2,000 blog posts later, podcasting has now become my go-to because it's very easy to create a ton of content with a single podcast interview.

Later on, we will explore how to repurpose your content so you get more bang for your buck. However, it's important to decide which format(s) you'll initially focus on when growing your authority platform.

Getting Clear On How You Will Spread That Content
Spreading your content is the key to gaining visibility. You should promote each new piece of content you produce to your community. That way, more people are bound to see it.

When you think about spreading your content, you have to get clear on two things:

#1: How you will promote each new piece of content to your existing audience

#2: How you can get other people to promote your content to their audiences

The reality of people who build authority platforms is that none of them did it alone (only the humble ones admit it). Did I write all of the blog posts, upload the YouTube videos, and interview people for my podcasts? Yes.

Did other people share my content? Did other people take the time out of their busy days to read my content for a few minutes? Did I learn from other people how to better spread my content so I could get on the right path to building an authority platform? Yes to all of those questions.

There are two ways most people build their authority platforms. The first way is that they optimize for the algorithm and get lucky with one piece of content that allows the entire brand to take off. You don't need a viral video with over 1 million views to have that effect. It could be just one video, blog post, or podcast episode that takes off for some reason, and that rising tide will lift everything else up higher.

It may look like these people grew their authority platforms by themselves, but that's not the case. To get that kind of success, you either did a ton of research and learned from other people, have a mentor guiding you, or an influencer pushed out that piece of content in a big way.

The second way people build their authority platforms is by building enough relationships and getting involved in enough joint ventures to the point where their audiences expand big-time. If you've ever noticed dozens of marketers promoting the same affiliate product (usually a training course), you've seen this in action.

Get the right people on your launch team and have the right offer in place, and you can get 10,000 email subscribers within 5 days (no exaggeration. I've been a part of these type of launches and the growth is incredible).

There are definitely things you have to do to grow your audience and start new relationships, but at the end of the day, you can only do so much as one person with one community. You'll need other people to help you, and the sooner you've got people spreading your content, the better.

You create that effect by building relationships and providing value. It goes back to why would people share your content in the first place. Some people will share your content because it was valuable. Others will share your content because your story strongly resonated with them. For the product launches, email marketers will share those offers because they can make money by sharing those offers and provide value in the process.

I promise I will share strategies and tactics later on, but for now I'm starting with the principles that go into building an authority platform. You can change the tactics and strategies, but you can't change the principles.

And if you don't know the principles, then you won't know how to apply the strategies and tactics for the best results.

Determine How You Will Make Money From That Content

If you do everything I've covered so far, you'll have a big community engaging with your content. Too many people don't emphasize money as much as they emphasize building the audience and getting big, pretty social media numbers.

There are some people who would rather make a consistent $1,000/mo with 100,000 social media followers than make a consistent $10,000/mo with 100 social media followers.

Note: for this example, assume everything else is equal such as same level of happiness, you do the work that you love full-time in both scenarios, etc.

I know this sounds ridiculous, and looking at it this way, who would turn down the consistent $10,000/mo in exchange for the big social media presence? You don't make money directly from social media (with the exception of Google Adsense for YouTube videos, but it's minimal for most people). You make money from social media by leading your community to the "money making" pages on your website.

It's easy to look at your social media numbers and just focus on beefing those up without thinking about how this makes more money. Just because you double your Instagram followers doesn't necessarily mean that you'll double your revenue. If you're going to grow on a social network, have a plan to make money with that social network.

You might be surprised to hear that there are some YouTubers with only 1,000 subscribers who make a full-time income. You might also be surprised to hear that there are some YouTubers with 10,000 subscribers who do YouTube part-time because they don't make enough money from their videos.

The YouTubers with full-time incomes but only 1,000 sub-scribers have a plan for making money with their videos. If you have the right offer at the right price point, you don't need too many clients to make a full-time income. If you charge $1,000/mo for a service, you only need 8 clients to make 6-figures (technically that puts us at $96,000/yr, but you get the idea).

Before you think about growth, think about how you're going to build up your revenue with your existing community. What type of value can you provide that would encourage your community to buy what you're offering? That's the question you have to ask yourself. Once you have the answer, incorporate that with the rest of your growth strategy.

The purpose of this first portion of the book is for you to think about the bigger picture. As I said a little earlier, the strategies and tactics can keep on changing, but these core truths are the foundation of any authority platform that makes it and doesn't fizzle out too early in the game.

Now we are going to get into the strategies and tactics for you to create content, spread your brand, and make money in the process.

Part 1

Everything Starts With The Offer

Twice a year, I go to the New Media Summit as what they refer to as an Icon of Influence. The Icons at the event are podcasters, and the attendees get an opportunity to make a pitch to all of the Icons in the room.

The entire event is led by Steve Olsher who is a leading expert in podcasting. In between pitching sessions, there are some educational sessions led by Steve or one of the speakers he invites to the event.

For me, one of the biggest takeaways from the educational sessions was that everything starts with the offer. Some attendees had questions as to what to name their podcasts. Steve's answer always gravitated to the current offer. If the attendee had a book, he'd recommend naming the podcast the same name as the book. He gave the same advice whether the attendee had a training course, service, or some other existing offer. Name the podcast after the offer.

It goes back to Steve's idea that everything should start with the offer. When you don't start with the offer, you're throwing a bunch of paint at a wall and seeing what sticks. When you start with the offer, you're utilizing a more sophisticated approach that allows the authority platform to turn into your full-time career.

When you start with the offer and keep it in mind, it's easier to avoid shiny objects that could lead you away from where you should be going. A new social network might come out, and while it's good to get on social networks when they are new, they're distractions if you don't stay focused on your offer.

If you want to branch out and talk about different topics, set up the offers before you talk about the topics. I will not go deep into a topic unless it's something I already have a product around or can coach people on.

The offer is what allows you to sustain the authority platform, and you can use the revenue from your offers to reach more people through advertising and partnerships.

How To Make Money With An Offer

At the end of the day, you make money with your offer when someone hands you money. People will only give you money if your offer fulfills a specific need. Getting clear on what these needs are and who has those specific needs is key to selling your offer.

Let's take toys as an example. Many kids will want the latest, hottest toy that everyone else seems to have. The toy companies run commercials showing the toy in action, and word of mouth plays a strong role too.

But toy companies don't make their money from the kids. The toy companies make their money from parents who buy the toys to make their kids happy. The kids act as a free salesforce army for the toy companies to get to their true audience...parents who want to make their kids happier via buying the toy.

Kids may want the toy, but they can't buy it themselves. The parents have the money, and you get to them through the kids...AND by making the toy likable from the parent's perspective. As a kid, I could like a certain toy or video game, but if my parents didn't want to get it for me, it wasn't happening. The same scenario plays out for 99% of the kids on the planet.

So the first step is to get clear on who is your ideal avatar. Many of the people who become my podcasting clients are authors who want to launch a podcast to attract more book readers.

Do I welcome clients who aren't authors or already have established podcasts? Of course I do. If they have a pain point I can fix, I know I can help them.

However, the majority of my podcasting clients are authors who want additional exposure…and podcasting is a great way for them to gain that exposure and boost their income at the same time.

It's not by accident that I know that many details about my ideal avatar. The more details you know about your ideal avatar, the more you can focus in on the people who you can help.

Too many people have their ideal avatar set as "human being with a pulse." With this avatar, you will never build an authority platform.

An authority platform is a platform focused on a specific authority. I help people launch, grow, and monetize their podcasts. If you want gardening tutorials from me, you're out of luck.

Should everyone start a podcast? I believe it makes sense. There's less than 1 million podcasts right now and the industry keeps growing each year. Compare that with the billions of blogs and numerous YouTube channels that already exist, and you'll realize that podcasting is a smaller pond with big opportunities.

Podcasting can also connect you with potential clients and famous people, and in my experience, I learn far more from interviewing people than reading books. It makes sense to start a podcast, right?

But not everyone is going to start a podcast. Some people don't care about building a brand. Others think podcasting is too much work. Some people may be successful already and not want to jump into podcasting. Others don't care about the opportunity podcasting provides and would rather just stay in the same rut they are in.

And even then, some people may not have enough money for your services.

Again and again, I talk with people who I know are good fits for my podcast coaching, but if they don't have the money, they can't be a client. Some people opt to lower their prices to get more clients, but it's harder to scale and serve everyone when you grow. The fewer clients I have, the better I can serve each one.

That's how I narrowed my search down to authors who don't have podcasts yet and want more publicity for their work. I could get even deeper into that avatar in the future and create a separate avatar that is just as effective.

You stick with your core avatar for your core offer, but each offer you create attracts a slightly different avatar.

One you figure out who your ideal avatar is, the next step is to determine where they hang out and how you'll engage with them. Toy companies run commercials, but you can also see them using Facebook and Google Ads to reach us on our devices. Depending on who your avatar is, the hang out location may be slightly different, but there are some common threads…

#1: LinkedIn is a great social network for business oriented brands. I've used LinkedIn to find guests for my shows, land a TEDx talk, and find prospects. I can filter the search so LinkedIn just shows me authors. Then it's up to me to determine if these same authors already have podcasts.

#2: Facebook Groups are a great place to interact with people who can become potential clients later on. Even if these people don't become clients, you will still be surrounding yourself with a community of people who represent your avatar. Depending on the group you're in, you can learn a lot and become a better person in the process.

#3: Industry events that attract your ideal avatar are one of my favorites. Talking with someone face-to-face is very different from emailing back and forth. The face-to-face relationships build up quicker and you get to truly know the people within your avatar. It's one thing to have a set avatar. It's something different to have specific people in mind when you think of the avatar. Having a specific person in mind also helps with selling.

Once you know your avatar and know where they hang out, the final step is to determine how you'll interact and what's the follow-up strategy.

Naturally, no one likes getting sold to, so reading off of a script or memorizing one that details why you and your offer are awesome won't work well. Organic conversations work the best, but you still need a way to start them.

Organic conversations almost always start with a question. The most common one you'll hear is, "What do you do?" or "How's your day going?"

Questions like those can get a conversation moving, but they're generic. The answers to those questions is automatic because we get them so often. What do you do gives me a minute description of what you do. Then the other person asks what you do. How's your day going usually ends up with "Good," or "Well."

The questions you ask control where the rest of the conversation goes. On Breakthrough Success, I frequently ask people about the habits that drive them to success. That gets me a very different response and conversation flow than if I decided to ask a guest to name their most embarrassing moment (something that, to date, I have never asked any guest and never will. Who really wants to answer that question).

If you want to get sales, you have to ask better questions. No salesperson I know asks for the prospect's most embarrassing moment of their life, but the questions you ask impact what direction the conversation takes.

Instead of asking people what they do, I ask people about what they're working on right now. That's my go-to question because it gives me a deeper sense of the current set-up and possible pain points. Here's an example of the difference between the two questions:

What do you do? — I'm a spiritual author who [does all of these things with spirituality, has accomplishments related to spirituality, helped clients with spirituality, etc]. How about you? What do you do?

What are you currently working on? — I wrote my book on spirituality and **am working to get it into the hands of as many readers as possible**. Right now my Facebook Group is loving the book and I have a bunch of social media posts queued up.

Notice that I bolded a pain point. That becomes important very soon. Before that though, I'll share possible ways I could respond to either of those questions (using the same example):

What do you do? — I help people launch, grow, and monetize their podcasts. [I share some more tidbits while thinking of how to steer the conversation forward. Most of these types of conversations fall flat after each person shares what they do or don't follow a good structure].

What are you currently working on? — Wow. It's impressive that you've got a Facebook Group going and all of the social media posts queued up. By the way, have you ever considered podcasting? I've written over 25 books and podcasting has worked very well for me to sell more books and make additional income.

In the first scenario, I say that I am a podcast coach and the person on the receiving end is passively listening.

In the second scenario, the person on the receiving end becomes an active participant in the conversation. The rest of the conversation leans towards follow-up questions and responses.

- When did you start podcasting?
- What is a podcast?
- How have you used podcasting to sell more books?
- You mentioned podcasting makes you income beyond selling books. How does that work?
- I'm interested in starting a podcast, but I've heard it is a lot of work. Is that true?

In my responses, I can shatter myths and demonstrate my expertise at the same time. I can shatter the myth about how much work podcasting is and explain the process. I can share how it's possible to make money from a podcast before you even launch your show and how to continue making money with your podcast after you've launched it.

The more opportunities you get to ask great questions to people who fit your avatar, the more likely you are to build an authority platform that produces a significant stream of income.

The Size Of The Authority Platform

It's easy to see a full-time YouTuber with over a million subscribers and think that's what you need to truly have an authority platform that makes you a full-time income. However, you don't need a large audience to have an authority platform.

You just need an audience of people who respect your work and support you so you can do said work full-time. The authority platform can grow over time and attract a larger audience, but sustainability matters more than size.

It's the reason why some people without social media followers make full-time incomes and some social networks like Vine go defunct. At its peak, Vine had over 200 million engaged users which is quite the audience, but it wasn't financially sustainable which is why it shut down.

It definitely sounds cooler to say you have 100,000 subscribers than 10,000 subscribers, but if you make more revenue and impact with the 10,000 subscribers, that's the model that makes more sense...and you can eventually grow 10,000 subscribers to 100,000 subscribers over time.

Size doesn't matter as much as impact, scalability, and sustainability.

What Offers Make Money?

So far we've talked about how sustainability is important and how everything goes back to the offer. We've cleared up a big myth about audience size and revenue generated.

Now we will jump into some of the different offers you can provide your audience to generate revenue for your business.

Each type of offer has its different perks, and the more different types of offers you can provide, the better.

To make things simple, start with the one area where you have the most expertise and people know you for your expertise in that area. You don't need a massive audience. Just enough people who know that you're an expert on the topic.

That's where you start.

Then you create an offer on that topic. Your second offer should be a different type of offer, but it should cover the same topic.

Earlier I mentioned my podcast coaching. However, that's not the only podcast related offer I have.

I also have a book called Podcast Domination, a training course called Podcast Promotion Blueprint, and a virtual summit called Profitable Podcasting Summit.

If I could go back, I'd use the same name throughout my offers but I liked different names at the time.

I also have offers around self-publishing, YouTube, virtual summits, content marketing, and many other areas. However, if you're just starting with your first few offers, theme them around your area of highest expertise.

The ideal offers vary from individual to individual, but these are the main ones for most people...

#1: Books — Pros don't just carry business cards. They also carry books. A book is a messenger that works while you sleep to build trust and introduce people to your other offers. Even fiction books fit that mold as you can conclude a fiction book by mentioning your other fiction works. Books can also generate a steady stream of income themselves from the book royalties.

#2: Coaching — You teach a person a certain skillset and get paid in exchange for your time. Coaching is a great model for reaching 6-figures. You can only take on a limited number of clients at a time due to time constraints, but you can change lives with coaching in a way that's harder to do with most of the other types of offers. You can also conduct group coaching sessions so you can coach more people with the same hour. You also have the potential to make more money with a group coaching hour than with a 1-on-1 coaching if you get enough group coaching clients. Remember to not underprice yourself if you become a coach. People aren't just paying for the 30-60 minutes they're with you. They're also paying for the years you invested in your craft and that level of expertise that you can bring to each coaching call.

#3: Training Courses — Books and training courses can go hand-in-hand. When you finish writing a book, you'll have an outline that you can very easily use to create the training course. Most books and training courses follow a similar teaching structure with most of the main content remaining the same. The difference is that some people prefer reading books while others prefer watching training courses. If you only have a book, you isolate the people who only watch training courses. If you only have a training course, you isolate the people who only read books.

#4: Services — Some people who are interested in launching a podcast tell me they're concerned about how much work goes into a podcast. They think about the editing, writing show notes, and finding guests to interview. That's why I also assist people with podcast management. Some people have no problem with launching their podcast and interviewing people, but the editing and show note writing can be a hassle. Some people who hear what you have to say will respond with, "That sounds good, but I don't have the time." You can offer done-for-you services that step in and say, "I'll do it so you don't have to worry about it."

#5: Virtual Summits — Gather around a bunch of influencers and interview each of them one at a time or in groups. Put all of those sessions into one portal that becomes known as your virtual summit. The speakers will proceed to promote the virtual summit and grow your audience. In return, attendees will learn more about each speaker, and speakers/affiliates receive a commission for each sale they make when promoting your virtual summit. Most virtual summits start out as free and then all of the sessions get put into a vault later on (only All-Access Pass Holders get lifetime access to the sessions). I also like to make my summits evergreen to continue attracting attendees.

#6: Sponsorship Placements — As you grow your authority platform, you can start incorporating sponsorship placements into your monetization strategy. I secure sponsorship placements for all of my podcasts and will continue incorporating sponsorship placements in the future. You can promise exposure to an audience of a certain size, placement in a book, a spotlighted session in a virtual summit, or something else. While a big audience helps, engagement is more important. The more creative you get with sponsorship placements, the better.

#7: Merchandise — Merchandise is underrated. When people buy your merchandise, you will live in their heads rent free. All someone has to do is put on your branded shirt, cap, hoodie, or something else…and they'll immediately think of you. You can offer merchandise with cool sayings, your logo, your slogan, or anything else that connects with your brand. And if you're going to ask other people to buy your merchandise, make sure you wear your own merchandise often… whether it be in public, at events, in your videos, or elsewhere.

You should pick one offer and create that before thinking about any of the others. If you try to work on all seven of these offers at the same time, you'll have difficulty with taking action and marketing your offers once you have them up.

When possible, connect the offers with each other so they do the marketing for you. For instance, in newer virtual summit videos, I have my books in the background. This subtle marketing turns some virtual summit attendees into readers. In my books, I'll share some of my offers at the end of the book to give them some extra exposure.

As a side note, the back of the book is your opportunity to share offers and places where people can continue following your work. This is the greatest opportunity that many authors miss because they don't think to put anything in the back of their books other than a conclusion and "About The Author" section. You can do something similar for training courses, coaching, and services.

There are other offers available depending on your niche, but these are the seven types of offers I see the most. The key is to focus on a few themes and have the offers connect with each other.

Now that we've talked a bit about the offer, the next part of the equation is the marketing. You know you have to create content to build the core of your authority platform, but if you create content without marketing that content, then you won't build up a platform.

This is why we will approach the marketing first. By constructing a solid marketing plan for each new piece of content you produce — and then implementing that plan — you have a much greater chance of building an authority platform.

Part 2

Expanding Your Tribe

Now that we have talked about the offer, the next step is to master marketing and know how you promote new offers, free content, and everything else that falls under your brand umbrella.

There are thousands of different ways to market yourself. Some are the tried-and-true methods that millions of people use. Others are the out-of-the-box ideas that position you in less competitive atmospheres that make it much easier for you to stand out.

The first step for any marketing strategy is to get clear on what your true goals are. It's easy to say you want to hit a certain follower number on each social network and put those as your marketing goals.

But those aren't your true marketing goals. The social media numbers themselves aren't the end. Social media is commonly viewed as a means to an end. You don't grow your social media followers and then do nothing with that audience. There's a reason behind the social media growth.

Some people grow their social media audiences because they want to get more blog traffic, podcast downloads, or video views.

So the true goal appears to be getting boosted traffic to your content, but we have to go even deeper.

Why do you want that traffic? Many people will say they want the traffic because it helps with their email list growth. So now the true goal appears to be email list growth.

But even then we can get a little deeper. Why do you want to grow your email list? Perhaps you heard that the money is in the email list and you want to attract more clients.

And why do you want more clients? Money.

The true goal of marketing is to make money. If you're investing in ads, influencer marketing, and other stuff, the true goal is to get an ROI.

Would you rather build up the social media followers and get traffic, or would you rather sell your offers to customers and clients? If you could sacrifice social media growth in exchange for more clients who stick with you over the long-term, would you do that?

Social media and traffic help you reach the end goal of more money in your pocket. But if you don't know what offers put the money in your pocket, and you don't know how you will move the relationship to the point of someone putting money in your pocket, you're shooting in the dark and hoping your shot goes in.

I don't like the idea of shooting in the dark when it comes to financial freedom. I like the idea of knowing and seeing my target in front of me.

Get clear on which offers will bring in money, and get clear on how you incorporate those offers within your marketing. That should be in the forefront of your marketing strategy… not the number of likes you get for your next post.

The principle behind every business' success is the ability to get traffic and turn it into sales. This principle makes it easier for you to apply the right marketing tactics and eliminate the ones that aren't yielding as high of a return.

For this part of *Build Your Authority Platform*, you will come across a variety of marketing tactics. All of these tactics work for getting more traffic…and hopefully more sales too. I only use the word hopefully because your ability to get sales boils down to how you present the offer.

Get To Know More People

At the end of the day, getting more traffic requires that a person comes across your content. Each of the tactics has a focus on starting a relationship that evolves into someone who visits your website and eventually becomes a client.

I make it a personal goal to interview at least 100 people each month. This boils down to about 25 interviews each week which is doable for my schedule. The reason I interview that many people is because it allows me to know a ton of people very quickly.

Not only do I get to know 100 new people each month, but each of those 100 people know a few people who I don't know yet. That comes to a total of 1,200 people who I'm interviewing each year. Assuming each person knows 5 people who I don't know but should know, that's an added 6,000 people who I could build a relationship with. Imagine the compounding overtime.

This is why I help my clients launch, grow, and monetize their very own podcasts and virtual summits. I help my clients start their own podcasts so they can interview people for their shows and grow their brands in the process. Interviewing people for your podcast or virtual summit is one of the easiest ways to talk with someone for 20-60 minutes depending on how long you want to make your episodes. Most of my episodes are around 20-30 minutes long.

Each week, my clients interview people who will promote the episode to their audiences for more episode. Some of these guests also turn into clients…all while growing a community of listeners.

I am able to publish 100 new interviews each month because I host multiple podcasts and evergreen virtual summits.

If you don't want to interview people, you can go to local events in your area. Use a site like MeetUp or Eventbrite to find nearby events. You can also participate in Facebook Groups and engage with people on those platforms. While online groups are also great, few things beat face-to-face meetings and talking with people in real-time on the phone or through an app like Skype or Zoom.

The more of the right people you know, the more you grow.

If you want to find that many people to interview, I recommend doing the following:

- **If you can, submit a query using a site like HARO**. You need your website's Alexa rank to be under 1 million. There are a variety of factors that go into the Alexa rank, but they boil down to traffic and user engagement.

- **Find people in Facebook Groups and invite them to be on your show**. Participate in these groups so people know who you are.

- **Use LinkedIn's people search feature** so you filter the search results to only show people who hold a certain position or job. You can use LinkedIn to specifically find non-

fiction authors who live in New York and speak English…
and that's only scratching the surface.

- **Browse through podcasts and virtual summits in your
  niche** and reach out to guests who have been featured on
  them. These guests know how guesting on a podcast
  works, and most guests say yes to every request that they
  get. High-profile guests may be less likely to say yes.

- **Go to local events**. Everyone naturally thinks about the
  speakers who could be great fits for your podcast, but don't
  overlook the attendees. I've gone to events where some of
  the attendees are just as incredible as the speakers.

Those are just five suggestions. There are some other tactics
that are similar such as searching through Twitter instead of
LinkedIn or searching through Amazon for authors in your
niche instead of searching through podcasts and virtual summits in your niche.

If you decide to pursue the interviewing route, those tactics
will give you more than enough guests to interview. If you do
a weekly podcast, you'll only have to publish 4 interviews
each month which means going all-in on just one of these tactics will present you with enough guests to interview.

The great thing about the interviewing route is that you can start and scale this method regardless of your audience size. You don't need a big audience or any audience to start attracting people to be on your podcast or virtual summit. Some people build their entire audiences by interviewing one person at a time.

The Strategy Behind Podcasting And Virtual Summits

In my book *Podcast Domination*, I explore a variety of business models around podcasting. For the purposes of this book, I will give you the basic concept of a strategy where podcasting and virtual summits give you added exposure.

The basic strategy is that you interview people who then promote the episode or summit depending on which approach you take. One big truth in business is that you can only do so much on your own. The sooner you can get other people to promote your brand for you, the sooner you will massively grow your audience.

Just make sure you have a way to convert your listeners into email subscribers because that's the best way for people to continue staying engaged with your brand. You can include a call-to-action at the beginning of your podcast episodes. For the virtual summits, I only let people attend the sessions if they register first (through this process, the attendee joins my email list).

One of the mistakes podcast and virtual summit hosts make is ceasing communication with the guest after the interview is published. I frequently keep in tabs with guests who have appeared on one of my podcasts or summits months after the interview is published.

Part of getting to know people is getting to know them over the long-term. If you make these relationships transactional, you are going to lose a lot of upside.

You can use podcasting and virtual summits to promote your offers and expand your business. From the marketing standpoint, you promote to your audience and your guests do the same.

Social Media Marketing — My Take Before I Share The Tactics

I want to first be clear that not everyone needs social media marketing. At least 90% of people need it for their businesses, but if you are already getting customers without social media marketing, it's not a need. Granted, social media marketing will help any business grow and reach more people, but if you are already a successful business and pursue social media at the cost of your entire foundation, don't pursue it.

The main weakness with social media marketing is the shiny object syndrome. We all know social media is one of the premier ways to grow a following and boost traffic. However, when you don't get results right away, it's easy to bounce around from social network to social network and keep yourself busy in the social media space without seeing much results.

The problem comes when we just see the act of posting as the result. Posting gives you the potential to see results. The results come in the form of engagement, traffic, and revenue. If you're not making revenue from your efforts, then the engagement and traffic are just "feel good" statistics that aren't yet doing much for the sustainability of your business.

The tactics I share will help you with getting engagement, traffic, and revenue from your social media marketing strategy. But understanding the context behind social media and how it relates to the sustainability of your business will allow you to make better decisions and focus on the numbers that matter the most.

Posting Frequency

On every social network, you have the ability to post new content. Not only do some people in your audience see your new posts, but those new posts increase your ability to get discovered by people who are outside of your audience. Hashtags started on Twitter and have since gone mainstream on virtually every social network.

It's best practice to include a few relevant hashtags in each of your posts to boost your post's discoverability. I like to mix a few popular hashtags with some more niche hashtags. The niche hashtags can help you get more discoverability and engagement sooner, and that engagement can help you get more discoverability for the more popular hashtag you include in your social media post.

Each social network has its different standards. While tweeting once an hour is standard practice, it's not something you see on Facebook. On Instagram and LinkedIn, it's good to post at least three times per day. On YouTube, you should start with a new video each week and build from there.

There are more social networks to choose from, and each social network will have its different guidelines. The funny thing about posting frequency is that there is no definitive answer. Every article has a different number. Some people will say that a single Instagram post each day is good enough while others prefer that you post on Instagram at least 5 times per day.

At the end of the day, the only posting frequency that matters is the one that works the best for your brand. Just because someone else is posting on Instagram 5 times per day and getting great results doesn't mean that's the best strategy for you. Your ideal posting frequency may be more or less than 5 Instagram posts per day.

To determine your ideal posting frequency, you have to start by being honest with yourself about what you currently can and cannot do. It's easy to look at someone like Gary Vaynerchuk and think you are immediately going to go from where you are now to becoming omnipresent on social media and posting daily content on all of those platforms.

When I saw Gary Vaynerchuk speak, I felt inspired to publish 10 new posts on LinkedIn each day. However, it only took two days for me to realize that the previously mentioned posting frequency wasn't the best one for me at the moment.

Will I ever post on LinkedIn more than 10 times per day? Maybe…but right now I'm not posting at that rate. Writing 10 posts each day would take considerable time away from other areas of my business where I need to be. I can write a post each day on LinkedIn and still get great results.

I do tweet once per hour because it's easy for me to schedule tweets using HootSuite's Bulk Scheduler. If I do post 10 pieces of LinkedIn content, it would probably be through something like HootSuite's bulk scheduler.

I see a higher ROI from writing books like this one, interviewing someone for a podcast or virtual summit, or coaching one of my clients. Social media posting is never meant to be the priority for your business. Social media posting is supposed to complement what you already do.

The goal is to post enough times across your social media platforms where you get the engagement but you can still work on the key areas of your business. As you grow your social media audience and get more engagement, traffic, and revenue, it makes sense to post content on the winning platforms more often.

This is why some YouTubers start with weekly uploads but then decide to upload 2-3 videos each week once their channels start taking off. There's a higher payoff in the additional video uploads now that you're seeing results.

If you continuously create new posts without optimizing them or doing what you can to make sure they get the most exposure, you'll have a bunch of posts that no one comes across. If you have zero subscribers, you should post new content, but you should invest more of your social media time to growing that audience than just posting.

The way to grow your social media audience on the actual platforms is to use the right hashtags and comment on other people's posts. Leaving meaningful comments on other people's posts is one of the easiest ways to grow your audience on social media. Just start with five thoughtful comments each day and build up as it makes sense.

Your current social media posting frequency is your baseline. You may want to add a little more to that baseline so you're active on a few other platforms…or not. Try different posting frequencies and see which social networks are getting you the best results. It is good to stay diversified while focusing most of your time on 1-2 social networks.

If you want to become omnipresent, delegate some of your social media tasks to others. It is very hard to be omnipresent if you do not have an assistant behind you. Rather than focus on being omnipresent, focus on getting the most out of the social networks that you're focused on.

Specific Tactics For Certain Social Networks

Posting frequency and engaging with people are two factors that apply to each social network. There are some specific tactics for certain social networks that will boost your edge. I'll share some of the different tactics that apply to each social network.

Twitter — follow targeted people in your niche who are likely to follow back. This is the tactic many people use to grow their audience. I have almost half a million Twitter followers in part because I follow hundreds of thousands of other accounts in my niche. When I follow more people, my blog traffic also grows.

Facebook — participate in a variety of groups. Engaging in these groups will result in some people within those groups reaching out to you. When it comes to a group experience and growing your business with groups, Facebook is unmatched.

Pinterest — start group boards so you get other people involved with your content creation. You can also create boards that appeal to different stages of your customer's journey. I have a Pinterest board of author resources to attract people who want to write their first book or people who want more exposure for their books. These are important features in a potential customer on my end because many of my podcasting clients are people who want more exposure for their books. You can also join other group boards with bigger audiences than yours to have an overnight audience. Vertical pictures win big-time on this platform.

YouTube — create a channel trailer telling people what your channel is about. Include a call-to-action in each of your YouTube videos so people subscribe and visit your website. For SEO, use VidIQ and TubeBuddy to figure out what keywords you should incorporate in your tags and descriptions. YouTube loves minutes watched and a high clickthrough rate, so it's important to create an attention grabbing thumbnail that leads to a high quality video experience people will want to watch from start to finish. You may also want to script your videos to the point of having a very detailed outline to make sure you stay focused and provide a great experience during the video. The outline is especially useful for knowing when to mention your calls-to-action for people to like the video, subscribe to your channel, comment, and go to your website. You don't mention all of these call-to-actions at the same time, but you script them into different parts of the video.

Instagram — post great pictures and comment on other people's pictures. Make it a point to post on Instagram Stories every day, especially when you want to push out a new piece of content. When you appear in someone's story feed, and they go through your stories enough times, you will be one of the first people your followers see in the stories tab. The stories tab appears above the feed of picture posts which gives you an opportunity to be seen more often on Instagram. Instagram stories can easily be put on your Facebook stories as well for added exposure.

LinkedIn — this is the best social network for getting to know business people on a one-to-one level. It's the preferred social network I use for getting clients and speaking gigs. Publishing consistent posts on LinkedIn about your expertise will make prospects more confident in their decision to buy your services because they can see that you know your stuff. LinkedIn's search filters are unmatched as I have hinted at before.

There are other social networks like TikTok and SnapChat to choose from, but many of those social networks have similar tactics compared to the rest of the social networks.

If you want to find a way to stand out on any social network, look at how users are currently using the platform and what is working in the moment. If you can ride on these trends, you can see a quick surge in audience growth, especially if it is a relatively new trend on a relatively new social network.

The One Tactic You Should Do Regardless Of The Social Network

With a variety of tactics comes a few winners. One of the best tactics for quickly growing your audience on any social network is to collaborate with other influencers. These collaborations have the potential to turn into mini partnerships where you're each sharing each other's content and getting featured in each other's content.

These scenarios allow you to get exposed to each other's audiences and experience boosted growth. That boosted growth can help give you a better ranking on the social network's algorithm which would result in a stream of new people visiting both of your accounts.

By collaborating with smaller but dedicated creatives, you'll grow your audience and open the doors to more collaborations and business opportunities. You can see the power of collaborations at any concert.

Almost no concert ever starts with the singer or the band you actually paid to see. If the concert has a start time of 7 pm, you can tack on at least an extra 30 minutes because 7 pm is usually when another singer or band is on the stage instead.

But as you wait for the singer or band you actually paid for, you might find yourself really enjoying the music from the singer or band playing before the lead act. I recently went to a concert and decided to follow a group of singers who performed before the lead act.

This group of singers didn't sell the thousands of tickets that were sold, but there they were singing to us. That's the power of collaboration. Perhaps they played a role in the event marketing and got the spot that way, but I am not sure.

What I am sure of is that they got extra followers that day. Attendees promoted them on their Instagram stories and the singers decided to share those people's stories. Upon some further research, I learned this group performed before the lead act last year as well.

The best collaborations are the ones that evolve beyond the one-off. This group of singers has multiple performances like these each year. Those group of singers have around 200 Instagram followers while the group we were there to see had around 2 million Instagram followers.

For most collaborations, you won't see that type of difference in social media followers. The group of singers with 200 followers were talented singers, so that likely played a factor in the decision making process.

It's better to build relationships with other creatives in your niche and eventually create content together. Almost every single big YouTube channel has collaborations at some point. The more collaborations the channel does, the faster it grows.

Finding collaboration opportunities just comes down to finding creatives with similarly sized audiences and reaching out to them one at a time. It is especially helpful but not required if the creative has done collaborations in the past.

In your outreach, just say how much you enjoy that creative's content and how you would like to collaborate on a new piece of content or promotion strategy to expand each other's audiences.

Creating content together would be like creating a video or blog post together. You cover some of the content and your collaborative partner covers the rest. You can also agree to promote each other's posts. This is common on Instagram where people do a shoutout for shoutout set-up. The end result is that each of you have larger Instagram followings. Do this with many people, and your Instagram account will soar.

Influencer marketing is one of the less utilized forms of marketing. Influencer marketing requires that you build relationships with other people, and the more long-term they are, the more your audience will grow.

Collaboration is a critical strategy you should employ for any social network you want to grow on. It's the foundation for any successful podcast or virtual summit. You could technically host a solo podcast, but if you're not interviewing people, you miss out on many of the benefits of hosting your own podcast or virtual summit.

A podcast can also be a great way to start a more long-term collaboration effort. You build more relationships with each interview, and you and the guest may decide you want to create more content together in the future.

In a collaboration, you both promote each other's content… so the more collaborations you get involved with, the more people will end up promoting your content.

Mention People In Your Content

We will soon talk about content creation. Creating content gives you something to market, but even in the content creation process, you can do some marketing.

There are a variety of reasons why people share content. Some people share a piece of content because they think it will be useful for their tribe. Other people share content because it relates to an opinion they hold onto strongly. Content gets shared because it's funny, entertaining, educational, on-point, and fascinating.

But there's another reason people share content. People love sharing content that they get mentioned in. People love sharing content that makes them look good.

Have you noticed that a business owner won't hesitate to mention if they've been featured in Success Magazine, the Huffington Post, or Inc Magazine? Have you noticed that every speaker that has done a TEDx Talk mentions it as one of their first things in their bio?

Doing so makes them look good. Some of us have small egos while others have unhealthy egos…but we all want to share and say stuff that makes us look or feel good.

If you mention a bunch of people in each piece of content you write…and then reach out to each person you mentioned, you're more likely to get people to share that content.

Before you create a new piece of content, think of at least 5 people who you can mention. Work those mentions into your outline and then make sure you reach out to the people who you mention.

There is some strategy involved with deciding who to mention and when. You don't want to mention the same person in every single piece of content you produce because they're not going to share every single piece of content you produce.

You also want to opt more towards creatives who have smaller but engaged audiences. These are the people who will actually take the time to read and respond to your message. If you mention a celebrity influencer, they're not likely to get back to you or share your content with their audiences.

Micro influencers are more likely to share your content with their audiences. Some micro influencers are always on the search for new content to add to their evergreen posting cycles. Each time a micro influencer adds your content to their evergreen posting cycle, you'll get a residual stream of traffic from that micro influencer.

The more people you mention in each of your new pieces of content, the greater opportunity you have to grow quickly.

One of the recurring themes of this book is to not view relationships as just one-offs. If you mention the influencer in your post, that influencer shares the post, and then the relationship ends there, you are missing out on a great opportunity.

Someone you mention in a post today can turn into a collaboration partner tomorrow. Some people have approached me and asked if they can become affiliates for my products. That doesn't happen if you have a bunch of one-off relationships.

I make it a point to go through my network and make sure I'm reaching out to people who know me at least once every six months. That is my bare minimum, but I like to reach out to once per month so they are reminded of who I am.

Whether it's me commenting on one of their social media posts, sharing an article I liked with the person, or letting them know about a new initiative, I let people see me at least once per month. And I comment on social media posts for a reason. Liking a post isn't enough to get noticed because that's everyone's default response. Fewer people comment, and when you do comment, you are likely to get a reply if the person is active on social media.

This is a very quick way to build a relationship. You'll build a healthy relationship quicker than interviewing the person for 20-30 minutes on your podcast. However, podcasting allows you to go deeper on these kinds of relationships and conversation beats email any day. It is best to leverage as many of these options as you can. The more you build and leverage relationships, the more you will grow your authority platform.

If You Have To Think About It, There's A Problem

When you create a new piece of content, how do you promote it in a way that builds your authority platform? If you have to think about it before taking any action steps, there's a problem.

In fact, if you have to think about your marketing before you do it, that could explain why your authority platform isn't as big as you'd like it to be.

One of the reasons content doesn't gain traction is because the creators behind that content don't fully tap into their authority platforms. If you see the person active on one social network but not active on the others, that's an example of a creative missing out on their authority platform's full potential. It's good to focus most of your efforts on 1-2 social networks, but you should still be active on the majority of your social networks.

If you are someone who has to think about your marketing before doing it, one of the best things you can do for your authority platform is to create a marketing playbook. When a new piece of content gets published, what happens?

Which social networks do you use to promote the new piece of content? How frequently do you post about it on each social network? Who do you reach out to when that new content gets published? How do you incorporate older content and future content that you haven't published yet? What is the end goal of the piece of content you're publishing?

The more detailed you get with your marketing playbook, the easier it will be for you to promote new pieces of content to your fullest potential. And the great thing about potential is that once you are working at your fullest potential, it doesn't take long for your ceiling to become your floor.

When you craft your playbook and get clear on all of the different ways you can be marketing your content right now, you free your mind to think of other thoughts. When your mind is free to explore, you get more creative and more opportunities start to appear in front of you. Many opportunities are right in front of us but we can't process them because we're thinking about all of the work we have to do. Having a clear mind is key to building an authority platform because you get to tap into marketing strategies and content experience few to none are utilizing.

Freeing my mind to explore is one of the reasons I'm able to launch multiple virtual summits each year. Virtual summits are one of the most incredible opportunities due to little to zero competition. This is my go-to strategy for growing my audience, building relationships, and boosting my income all at the same time.

Something like a virtual summit launch can sound like an intense effort, but if you clear your mind, a virtual summit isn't as difficult to pull off. Sure, you have to interview at least 20 people for your virtual summit, but if you do 2 interviews each week, you have all of the interviews done in under 90 days. This makes it possible for me to launch a new virtual summit every quarter.

You should delegate at least 30 minutes each week to thinking about your marketing playbook and different opportunities you can explore that you haven't explored yet. Virtual summits have been a boon for my business, and I have helped others get started through my Virtual Summit Blueprint course and group coaching.

You will be amazed at what you think of if you take the time to think of new ideas for 30 minutes each week.

Part 3

Content Creation Strategies And Hacks For Success

Your content forms the backbone of your brand. Without content, there's nothing for you to market and monetize. I decided to make content creation the last part of the book because too often people put on their creative hats without thinking of what the objective is and how each new piece of content will translate into more sales.

For this part of the book, I'll share some ways you can create content quicker and translate new content into more sales for your business.

The Different Types Of Content

There are a variety of ways to publish new content. You can publish new content as blog posts, videos, podcast episodes, and pictures. Those are the four formats you'll see the most often. There are other ways to publish your content such as a

SlideShare, but for the purposes of this book, we will focus on those four formats.

When clients ask me which content format they should focus on, I tell them to create content around all of those formats. The reason you want to create content for all of these formats is because people have different ways of learning and consumption.

Some people like to learn by reading. Others like to learn by watching or listening. The same goes for entertainment. Some people have no problem reading a long joke posted online while others want to see a comedy skit on YouTube. Some detective stories are exclusively podcasts. You may prefer to read about it or watch an episode on TV, but some people prefer to listen to them on podcasts.

Here's the point. If you are only actively creating content for one of these formats, you will miss out on all of the people who have a different style of content consumption. There are some people who will only watch training courses and never pick up a book. In that scenario, if I only write the book, I'm leaving a ton of money on the table.

If I'm only active on YouTube but don't bother with launching my own podcast, I'm losing out on the growing segment of podcast listeners. As a side note, there are only around 750,000 podcasts at the time of writing which makes them much less saturated compared to other options. In any event, it is essential to produce new content for all of the big four formats.

How To Produce That Much Content

Business owners understand how important it is to produce content for all of these different formats because it expands their reach. However, many people balk at the idea of producing that much content because of the time commitment.

On the other side, you have creatives who will create content for all of these formats but not consider how they will make money from all of this effort. I'm all for creating content for all of these formats, but if it doesn't make you money, you have a hobby and are missing out on incredible opportunities.

The two secrets to producing that much content is to come up with the best ideas and repurpose them…and to do collaborations. On some days, I interview 10 people for future podcast episodes and virtual summit sessions. If you launch a weekly podcast, you'd only have to interview 1-2 people each week to keep up, but since I have a bunch of podcasts and virtual summits, I interview 10 people on some days.

Knowing that someone is waiting on the other side gives you an extra sense of commitment to create new content with the help of the podcast guest or summit speaker.

When each interview gets published, I turn some of the soundbites into Instagram and Pinterest pictures and share them on my other social networks. Some of the ideas from each episode turn into blog posts or YouTube videos.

You can even write a blog post and turn it into a YouTube video or vice versa. Since no one will remember all of the content you create, there is no limit to how much you can re-purpose the same ideas. You can write a blog post and turn it into a YouTube video a month later. Three months from now, you can take that same YouTube video and turn it into a blog post.

You can then take that blog post and put it in one of your books or put the YouTube video into one of your training courses. And we didn't even mention podcasting in this example.

Some people will listen to the podcast version of a content idea but not read the blog post version of that same content idea. Some people will consume both pieces of content and get the same value twice. It serves as a good reminder for people who remember both pieces of content.

With that said, it is important to realize that most people will forget your content about a week after consuming it. They may remember what it did for them or the impact you had, but people are too busy and inundated by other people's content to remember everything.

In fact, it should be your duty to continue bringing up your best content that has the most value.

I bring all of this up because some people get a bad feeling about taking a YouTube video and turning that same video into an audio file for their podcast. By repurposing your top content (in terms of value and profitability), you are continuing to serve your audience and grow your business at the same time.

The Best Content Format To Kick Off The Repurposing Cycle

By far, the best type of content to create from a repurposing standpoint is video content. When you create video, you talk, and we all talk much faster than we type. You can then take the best ideas from your video and combine them into a blog post. Some people simply embed their video into the blog post with a transcript underneath.

You also create audio content by talking. However, the only problem with audio content is that it's harder to repurpose into video. Sure, you can have a static background for your video, but it won't be as engaging as a slideshow or people seeing you in the video. Video is simply the easiest content format for repurposing into other content formats without too much additional work.

Creating Content VS Marketing Your Content

A never-ending debate amongst people in the space is how much time should be spent creating new content versus how much time should be spend marketing that content.

This is a chicken or the egg scenario because you can't market any content unless you create content, but you don't have a business unless you are marketing your content. Content creation doesn't even always go first. You can promote a product launch and do the marketing for that offer before you create any of the content.

When I offer one of my books for preorder, it means that I am nowhere near finished with that book and use the preorder deadline as a hard deadline. I get sales for my product before I start creating it.

If you do a preorder using Kindle Direct Publishing, you are obligated to complete that book. If you do not complete the book and submit it to Kindle Direct Publishing in time, you lose the ability to offer your books for preorder for an entire year.

For authors who want to make it on bestselling lists and give their books a massive head start, not having the preorder capability would be a huge blow to that goal. That's why completing the book before the deadline becomes important and urgent as it gets closer.

However, if you offer a training course for preorder on your own platform, and it doesn't make any sales, you are not obligated to create that training course. Why create something that no one has expressed any interest in?

For this scenario, the marketing allowed you to save hours of time that would have went into creating new content for the course. I'd rather do the marketing first and get no sales than create all of the content and then get no sales with the marketing. Granted, none of those options are ideal, but the former allows you to save time and quickly direct your efforts elsewhere.

This is one of the many reasons why the debate about how much time we should spend creating versus marketing content is so prevalent.

Now that I have shared why this is such a big topic, I'm going to share some of the rules I use when it comes to allocating time for creating content and marketing that content.

The first rule is that you are not allowed to create more content than you can market. If you upload a video each day but you can't properly promote all of them to your community, you have to scale back on content creation. If this is you, proceed to upload 1-2 videos each week so you have more time to promote each video.

If you find that you're getting a small number of views, producing higher value content isn't the answer. Higher value content just keeps the people who you get more engaged with the content, and some of those same people may share your content. If you actually want to drive people to your content, the answer is more marketing.

If you can upload a new video each day and properly market each of them, then congratulations…you can continue to create daily videos. Granted, it is usually more effective to market fewer pieces of content over several days than to do mostly one-off marketing for new content you publish if you are on a daily schedule.

The second rule is that you must find ways to get into the gray area of content creation and content marketing. Earlier, I explained why mentioning other people in your content is a great idea. When you mention other people in your content, you are creating more content and providing more value. At the same time, you have a few people you can reach out to and say that you mentioned them in your content. When it comes to the creation VS marketing debate, few options beat the gray area where you get to do both in a single action.

The third rule is that when your marketing is automated and performing very well, create more content. While this rule doesn't apply to most people, it can apply as you create more content and grow a large audience. On YouTube, when a creator gets very successful, YouTube will push out their videos to their audience for them. YouTube essentially does most of the marketing for these creators.

In the scenario, you should add an extra video each week to your schedule if you can. The closer you can get to daily, the more habitual it will be for people to consume your content. I only recommend this course of action when a platform like YouTube, online advertising, or something else is essentially doing the bulk of the marketing for you.

The reason I'm writing more books is because I know I can plug each new book into Amazon Book Ads and Amazon will do the marketing for me over the long-term. I just make a big announcement on the day the book gets launched. This isn't a good strategy if you want to launch a signature book that becomes a New York Times bestseller or something like that, but for the Amazon Book Ads approach, the more books, the better.

If Amazon Book Ads weren't a thing and I had to market each of my books without Amazon's help, I would publish fewer books and plan out the marketing campaigns several months in advance.

The fourth rule is to think about the money. If you made $100 for each piece of content you published (affiliate sales, selling your own products, etc.), how much content would you create?

I'd say that you would do everything you could to produce daily content as long as you could maintain $100 per piece of content and still do the marketing.

However, what if you could up that number to $1,000 for each piece of content you create. Rather than create new content each day in this scenario, you just have to create 3 new pieces of content each month to make the same revenue as the former example. Granted, I'd definitely produce more than 3 pieces of content each month if that was my number. However, to reach those numbers, it may be necessary to produce less content so you have more time to promote your most profitable pieces of content.

Many people make this kind of money from free content they produce by promoting an offer and attracting people to that piece of content. You can email your list and promote on social media, but many of the bloggers performing very well use Google and Facebook Ads to drive more traffic to their most profitable blog posts.

Similarly to how your top 10 pieces of content will make up the bulk of your traffic, your top 10 profitable pieces of content will make up the bulk of your revenue associated with free content. These winners are the ones you should concentrate on the most with evergreen promotions and Google and Facebook Ads.

The fifth rule is to have plans and deadlines for content creation and content marketing. Each day, you should know exactly what you have to do on the creation side and on the marketing side. Create a calendar for your typical week and allocate times for each part of the process. That way, you will stay focused on both the creation and the marketing sides of your content.

Most people would benefit if they spent more time marketing their content than creating new content. Creating too much new content can overwhelm people, and promoting new content each day can make some of your marketing efforts feel rushed. If you market fewer pieces of content, you are likely to boost your traffic and revenue. It is better to create a new piece of content each week that gets 100 visitors than it is to create new content each day and average 10 visitors for all of that content.

Using The Socratic Outline To Lengthen Your Content And Make Money

One of the most common tactics people will recommend around content creation is to create an outline. An outline gives you a clear path of how your content will flow from start to finish. Granted, most outlines aren't perfect and you may deviate from an outline at certain points. The outline is simply a guide that allows your mind to think in a more creative way. Rather than thinking about what you'll cover next, you can think about how you'll enhance the content you're producing because you know the structure.

Earlier I mentioned that it is important to think about how much money each piece of free content will produce. This is where a Socratic Outline can help.

In a Socratic Outline, you do your typical outline. Write the title of the new piece of content you want to create and list some talking points. Under each talking point, I want you to put yourself in your avatar's shoes and think of what questions they would have.

In one of my YouTube videos where I explained <u>the math behind making $100,000/yr from dividend investing</u>, I thought of some questions my audience would have. Some people would wonder if it was possible for them if they were older. Other people would have the misconception that for a dividend stock yielding a 3% dividend that you would need $3.3M to make that much money from dividend investing (I talk about the growth rate and DRIP in the video which explain why you can reach a goal like $100,000/yr from dividend investing sooner than you think).

Think about what types of questions your content consumer would have, write those questions in your outline, and then answer them in your content. This is the foundation of a Socratic Outline.

However, one of the questions you should include in your Socratic Outline should be, "How will this piece of content make me money?"

At the end of the dividend investing video, I showcase a few of my books that I have published on Amazon. At the time of writing, I'm new to talking about dividend investing and don't quite yet have an array of products around it. However,

I chose to promote some similar products while I work on some dividend investing related products for the future.

For instance, my next book project will be on how you can retire early through dividend investing. Once I complete that book, I'll be promoting that book in future videos. It might be out right now as you are reading this. If not, you can expect it very soon.

Getting people on your email list is important, so you should incorporate a call-to-action for each piece of content you create which directs people to join your email list. If you are promoting an affiliate product, you can tell people that you'll offer some exclusive training or other perks for people who join through your link.

That way, not only do you make more money, but you also grow your email list at the same time. That is a win-win of epic proportions for any content strategy. People who spend money with you once are more likely to spend money with you in the future, and the money is in the email list and follow-ups.

The Socratic Outline allows you to lengthen your content and think of how you want to incorporate calls-to-action throughout your content. Lengthier content keeps a content consumer's attention over a longer period of time even if they are just scrolling through a blog post.

The longer you can keep someone engaged with your content, the more you will be rewarded by Google and YouTube. The algorithms will decide to give you additional exposure that will compound over time. This is why most of the blog posts that rank on the top of Google are at least 2,000 words. Some of these same blog posts are over 10,000 words, but I'd rather write a book with those 10,000 words because that works for my strategy. I know how to market a book with Amazon Ads and understand that model better. 2,000 words on the other hand is lengthy but doable for a blog post.

If 2,000 words works for you and you can reach 3,000 words, you can experiment with it. The few people writing 10,000 word blog posts are doing so because for them it is a proven concept. They've seen great results from these ultra lengthy blog posts and will continue producing them.

A good rule of thumb is that the more time you spend creating a single piece of content, the more time you should spend marketing that same content. It would be a shame if a 2,000 or 10,000 word blog post you went all-out on only got a few visitors. Intense marketing prevents that problem from happening.

Free Content VS Paid Content

We've talked about how you can make money with each free piece of content you produce. Promoting affiliate offers doesn't require that you create any of your own paid content. Just make money with the affiliate offers and keep them coming.

However, it is also good for you to have some paid content such as a book or a training course. Some people in your tribe will love you but not want to buy your affiliate offers. And if you promote affiliate offers over $100, not everyone in your community will buy.

Remember, it doesn't matter how much money someone spends with you. Even if they just spend $1 on a product or service that you promote, they are more likely to spend more money on your products, services, and recommendations later on.

An inexpensive Kindle book is a great starting point for many people who don't have the means to afford my coaching or the affiliate products I recommend. If you create free content but don't create any paid content, then you are leaving a lot of money on the table. On the other hand, if you only create paid content but no free content, people won't buy from you. People will view your paid content as an upgrade from the free content they have been consuming. Without any free content for content consumers to determine whether your paid content will be any good or not, they are less likely to buy your paid content.

Think of it this way. Imagine someone selling a podcasting course about how to launch, grow, and monetize a podcast. The plot twist? This person doesn't even have a podcast or gates all of their podcast episodes for people who will pay for access to the episodes. The reason I offer podcasting related products and services is in part because I currently host three podcasts.

People who like the episodes and my interviewing style may decide to buy some of my products and services. People who don't like the episodes probably won't buy my products and services. Either scenario is okay, but the podcast episodes paint a better picture of who I am and my level of expertise in the podcasting industry.

So now the question becomes how much time should I spend creating free content and how much time should I spend creating paid content. This answer, more so than the creating versus marketing argument from earlier, varies from person to person.

If you want to create a signature product, then once you create that signature product, you don't need to create paid content for a while. After you create the signature product, you can focus most of your content creation efforts on creating free stuff that still ends up making you money and leading people to the signature product.

If you want to create a variety of paid products, and you can successfully get sales for those paid products, then focus more of your time on paid products. A new piece of free content for each format each week will be sufficient in this scenario. I prefer to create a ton of books with Amazon Book Ads set up for each one than have one signature book that I pour a few years into. This model involves you creating much more free products but is less risky.

If one of my books doesn't do well, I can always move on and write another one. I also have the option to relaunch certain books which I believe have potential to be performing better. If a signature book didn't do well, that would be more bothersome because a signature book is an all eggs in one basket type of model. Sometimes it works spectacularly while at other times it does not.

The advantage with creating an array of products is that you get to learn from mistakes more quickly. I crunched the numbers on my books and saw that two of my relatively newer books accounted for over 50% of my book royalties. I reached that point with those two books because of all of the other book launches I had done before. Now my newer book launches get an instant edge because of my past experiences and what I'm doing now.

The book before this one, YouTube Decoded, jumped off to a fast start and the sales keep on coming. It is already on its way to becoming one of my top earning books later down the road. When you master the launch and can use something like Amazon Book Ads to promote your offer, it's a matter of how many products can you create that can work with the model you are currently using.

The free versus paid content choice depends on how much content creation you can handle. Weekly free content for each of the formats is the very minimum, and as you create more paid products, you will learn from your mistakes to ensure your next launch is more successful.

Create Content Around The Ideas Your Audience Recommends

One of the easiest ways to grow your brand is to acknowledge the people in your audience. When someone leaves a comment, I respond as quickly as I can. This increases the likelihood of that person consuming more of my content.

As you get more comments, some people in your audience will ask you to create content around specific topics that are relevant to your niche. These are the topics you have to quickly jump on.

When you create content based on your audience's recommendations, your audience will come to appreciate you taking the time to engage with them, and you'll likely get more comments on future content.

An extra bonus is to shout out the person who came up with the content idea. That way, you encourage your audience to engage with your content and frequently visit your YouTube channel, blog, podcast, and social networks.

Granted, you should still think about how this content will make you money so its a profitable effort. That is why you should only pursue ideas related to your niche instead of far out ideas that may be a better fit on someone else's platform.

In addition to boosting your audience's engagement with your content, you will also be creating content that your audience wants more of. This will increase the number of visitors who fit within your avatar while increasing retention.

The better you can engage with your audience and do things for them, the more engaged they will be with your work. They'll also share your work with other people who may fit within your avatar.

Cross Promote Your Different Content Platforms
Some people may enjoy your YouTube channel but have no idea that you have a podcast or blog. These people may watch videos, listen to podcasts, and read blog posts. However, they won't consume any of your additional content if they don't know about the other content you're producing.

This is why it is so important to cross promote past content that you have published in other formats. When you create new content, think of your previous content that is similar to the new content idea. The most successful brands are the ones that bounce people back and forth from one platform to the other.

Some people who watch my YouTube videos listen to my podcast episodes. Some of these same people read my blog posts and engage with my social media posts. As these people see my content more often, the trust between us builds deeper.

Cross promotion also increases the likelihood of people continuing to consume your content over extended periods of time. At the end of a YouTube video, YouTube will display suggested videos that may or may not be your videos (in most cases, YouTube displays videos from other creators). Places like YouTube are also continuously recommending other people's content. That way, if someone doesn't like a video, there's another option readily available.

While this is a great perk for consumers, it makes the creative process more challenging. This is a great feature for creatives when their video shows up as a suggestion after someone else's video. However, when someone clicks away from your video, podcast episode, or blog post, you might lose that person forever.

The way to keep people engaged in your brand is to keep giving them content to consume and keep directing your audience to relevant content that can help or entertain them.

Eventually, people remember you by your name rather than by chance (i.e. showing up as a recommended video VS someone typing your name in a search engine). When people remember you by your name and work, that's when the authority platform is in full effect.

Cross promotion is different from repurposing. In a repurposing scenario, you do a video interview and publish it to YouTube. You then take that same video interview and turn it into an audio file for your podcast. You take that video or podcast episode and embed it in your blog post with either a brief description or a transcript.

In a cross promotion scenario, you record a podcast interview on how to become a bestselling author. Later on, you create a YouTube video containing 5 tips to finish writing your book. At the end of the video, you can say something like, "Now that you know how to finish writing your book, if you want to become a bestselling, listen to this interview I recently published on my podcast. The link will be in the description."

Your final call-to-action should be for people to engage with you on the platform they are on, for them to join your email list, or for them to buy one of your products. At any point before that final call-to-action you can mention some of your older pieces of content. This creates the potential of taking the content consumer down a rabbit hole where they learn a lot about your work and story in a short period of time.

Reviving Old Content

One of the biggest mistakes content creators make is neglecting their older content and exclusively focusing all of their efforts on newer content. Part of content creation is to create additional content that provides value to your audience. Part of that definition is going back to a past piece of content and providing additional value.

Not all content is worth reviving, but if you revive the right pieces of content, you can see a surge in traffic and sales. A good place to start with reviving older content is to look at your Top 10 Lists.

Your first Top 10 List should be based on popularity. Giving some love to the content on this list can revitalize content on the Top 10 List that may have been falling off. You can also link to some of your newer content in your most popular content to give your new content a boost.

Your second Top 10 List should be based on how much revenue each piece of content generated for your brand. Revitalizing one of these blog posts can give you an extra edge on search engines. With these pieces of content, I recommend that you approach it with more care as changing it too much can risk hurting the conversion rates.

For both your most popular and most profitable pieces of content, using them as good models for future work will make it easier for you to see further success down the road. Popular content should be frequently revised while profitable content should occasionally get tweaked. However, if a once profitable piece of content is now not making you any money, it's worth making some tweaks to bring back that revenue.

Finding your most popular pieces of content shouldn't be too difficult. WordPress, YouTube, and most podcast hosting sites allow you to rank your content by popularity over a certain time period. You then go through the list of that most popular content and see who you biggest winners are.

Finding your most profitable pieces of content is a bit more challenging since there isn't a built-in metric for that. The approach for finding the most profitable pieces of content is to track clicks and total sales of the products you promote. If one of your blog posts drives twice as many clicks to a product as your typical blog post, that's a stat worth focusing on.

Twice as many clicks to a product doesn't ensure the blog post made more revenue, but it's helpful to know and very likely led to more revenue.

Another factor with measuring a piece of content's profitability is what product is being promoted. When I promote one of my books, I stand to make a little less than $3 per sale as a worst case scenario.

I could sell 100 copies of my Kindle books from a single blog post, but it still wouldn't match up to a single ThriveCart sale from my "11 Ways To Use ThriveCart To Get More Sales From Your Website" blog post. ThriveCart currently pays me $345 for each sale.

From a make money standpoint, I'd rather sell ThriveCart once than sell 100 Kindle editions of my books. Granted, I make additional money when people read my books (i.e.

some readers buy another book of mine, something I recommend, etc.), but on a basis of book royalties alone, I'd have to sell almost 150 Kindle editions of my books to make the same money as selling one package of ThriveCart.

That is another factor to consider when measuring the profitability of each piece of content.

When it comes to actually reviving the piece of content, here are some things you can do...

- Increase the length of the content
- Add more links to your content and other people'e content
- Put in affiliate links each time you mention a tool or resource when applicable
- Add more pictures and other media to the old piece of content
- Link to it in pieces of content you create in the future — don't forget about it
- Insert a stronger call-to-action
- Enhance SEO

It is always good to go back to your top performing content and give it new life. If you try to go back to all of your old pieces of content and try to revive all of them, you'll be wasting a lot of time. Only some content is worth reviving. Extra time can be allocated towards creating new content and doing other things to build your authority platform.

Re-uploading an updated video is not an option for YouTube. The only way you can change your older videos is by changing their descriptions. This can still help provide a better experience and improve your SEO ranking in the process. Many of these tactics still apply to YouTube videos, but you won't be able to add length to the video since you can't re-upload.

Content Creation On The Road

The final topic we'll cover for content creation is how you can create content on the road. This is often a missed opportunity for creatives who may do most of their work sitting at home looking at a computer.

While I'd rather work on a computer, you can also create content on your smartphone. This is one of the best content creation opportunities because you can create content during every waking minute (I'd never do that, but it is possible).

Content creation on the smartphone creates possibilities in a variety of circumstances where a computer is impractical. Some people record videos and audio while driving. While I don't do this myself (let's start with me getting a license), several creatives can drive and create new content safely. All you have to do is set up your smartphone somewhere, hit record, and position it on the side. That way, you're not looking at the camera and you never have to.

If you get distracted while creating content like this, it's not worth it. However, if you drive a lot and can do it just fine, it is a tremendous opportunity to create new content in time normally spent surfing the radio.

If you are in transit on a bus or subway, this is your opportunity to write the next blog post or at least outline it. Too many people use these types of moments to mindlessly scroll through their social media feeds.

Just because you aren't at home in your video set-up doesn't mean you can't create videos while you travel. In fact, it's a good thing to create videos while traveling because it gives people a different side of you. The more different sides you give, the more people come to know, like, and trust you.

The more content you create on the road, the more time you have to market and monetize that content.

Conclusion

Building an authority platform requires revenue for sustainability and an audience for expansion. When done with a purposeful content creation strategy, new content will aide you with these two critical objectives.

To build an authority platform with a solid foundation, it is important to focus on the offer and work your way down. Get clear on the key objectives of your business and how you will reach them.

It is possible for anyone to build an authority platform. There are no short cuts. Only inputs and outputs. The more time you input in the right areas, the better the outputs. The more money you input into the right ads, the better the output.

Now it is up to you to create your own authority platform. You have the knowledge you need to get started and build on what you already have. All that's left is the implementation and experimentation along the way.

About The Author

Marc Guberti is a USA Today and WSJ bestselling author with over 100,000 students in over 180 countries enrolled in his online courses. He is the host of the Breakthrough Success Podcast and Radio Show where listeners learn how to achieve their breakthroughs. He coaches content creators on how they can attract more traffic to their content and boost revenue.

If you enjoyed this book, make sure you subscribe to my YouTube channel (just search "Marc Guberti" on YouTube) for videos that will help you gain more visibility and revenue with the content you're creating.

Marc's Other Books

Are you looking for your next book? If so, Marc has written over 20 books which can all be found on Amazon. Here's some of what is waiting for you if you search "Marc Guberti" on Amazon…

<u>Content Marketing Secrets</u> — Discover the key secrets for getting massive traffic and revenue

"This book is a getting-it-done guide for going big in small, manageable steps. Marc has put the playbook together for you." --**Andy Crestodina, author of Content Chemistry**

<u>Podcast Domination</u> — Discover the ultimate podcasting strategies that will help you launch, grow, and monetize your show

"Thorough coverage of the subject. Many books in the topic seem to be teasers to sell premium content. This book is not like that - he covers all topics." — **Amazon Review**

<u>The Wealthy Author</u> — Discover how to use books to grow your brand and earn passive income.

"If you want to learn more about making more with your books, this is the book you need!" — **Michelle Kulp, bestselling author**

<u>YouTube Decoded</u> — Discover how to create engaging YouTube videos that attract visibility and revenue to your business.

"YouTube is a mystery to many and thanks to Marc's tenacity and in-depth focus on education, YouTube Decoded is the book that really helped our team to understand the power of the platform. Well written, worth picking up." — **Mark Asquith, founder of Rebel Base Media**

www.ingramcontent.com/pod-product-compliance
Lightning Source LLC
Chambersburg PA
CBHW020559220526
45463CB00006B/2367